Remember the Ladies

Remember the Ladies

A Story about Abigail Adams

by Jeri Chase Ferris
illustrations by Ellen Beier

A Creative Minds Biography

Carolrhoda Books, Inc./Minneapolis

*For three of my favorite ladies—Cheryl, beloved
daughter-in-law, and Shanna and Rebekah, beloved
granddaughters   —J.C.F.*

For Laura Curtis   —E.B.

Text copyright © 2001 by Jeri Chase Ferris
Illustrations copyright © 2001 by Ellen Beier

This book is available in two editions:
Library binding by Carolrhoda Books, Inc.,
a division of Lerner Publishing Group
Soft cover by First Avenue Editions,
an imprint of Lerner Publishing Group
241 First Avenue North
Minneapolis, MN 55401 U.S.A.

Website address: www.lernerbooks.com

Library of Congress Cataloging-in-Publication Data

Ferris, Jeri.
    Remember the ladies : a story about Abigail Adams / by Jeri Chase
Ferris ; illustrations by Ellen Beier.
        p.   cm. — (A creative minds biography)
    Includes bibliographical references and index.
    Summary: Chronicles the life and achievements of the nation's second
First Lady and advocate for women's rights.
    ISBN 1-57505-292-X (lib. bdg. : alk. paper)
    ISBN 1-57505-558-9 (pbk.)
    1. Adams, Abigail, 1744–1818—Juvenile literature. 2. Presidents'
spouses—United States—Biography—Juvenile literature. 3. Adams, John,
1735–1826—Juvenile literature. [1. Adams, Abigail, 1744–1818. 2. First
ladies. 3. Women—Biography.] I. Beier, Ellen, ill. II. Title. III. Series.
E322.1.A38 F37 2001
973.4'4'092—dc21   00-008090

Manufactured in the United States of America
1 2 3 4 5 6 – MA – 06 05 04 03 02 01

Table of Contents

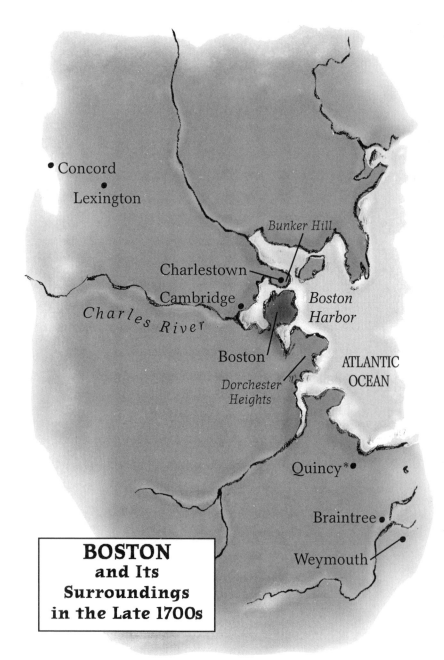

Concord
Lexington

Bunker Hill
Charlestown
Cambridge
Charles River
Boston Harbor
Boston
Dorchester Heights
ATLANTIC OCEAN
Quincy*
Braintree
Weymouth

**BOSTON
and Its
Surroundings
in the Late 1700s**

The northern part of Braintree was renamed Quincy in 1792. This was where John Adams was born and grew up, and where John and Abigail lived when they were married.

Introduction

Abigail Adams was born over 250 years ago in the colony of Massachusetts, one of thirteen British colonies in North America. Abigail, like most people who lived in the colonies, was a citizen of England. There was no United States of America—not yet.

The colonists were ruled by the king of England, George II, and followed English rules and laws. These laws were different for women than for men. Women could not vote, could not govern, and could not own anything. Men did all the voting, governing, and owning. Men made the laws, too.

But Abigail thought women should not be ruled by laws they did not make. Women are the equal of men, she said. Men should not have "such unlimited power."

Despite all Abigail's talking and writing, when she died in 1818 women still could not vote, govern, or own property. Abigail Adams changed history in another way. Through her work, her ideas, and her letters, she enabled her husband to help create a new country: the United States of America. And through those letters, she shows us what people thought, felt, and did in colonial America as the world changed around them.

1

A Wild Beginning

"Wild colts make the best horses," her grandmother said cheerfully, when Abigail acted wild. But Abigail's mother feared she would turn out badly.

Abigail *tried* to look like a proper young lady—she pulled her dark hair back smoothly and tied it with a pink ribbon. She dressed in her best apron and kerchief. It didn't work. She listened with wide eyes when a neighbor warned her that she would be either a very good or a very bad woman when she grew up.

Abby did want to be good when she grew up. In the meantime, she was busy making up her own mind about things, and telling people (even men) what she thought.

Abigail Smith was born in November 1744, in Weymouth, Massachusetts, a tiny seaport and farming town ten miles south of Boston. Her father, William Smith, was the town's minister, so he baptized her himself when she was only one week old.

By the time Abigail was eight, she begged to go to a real school like her seven-year-old brother, William, or even to a Dame school, taught by a woman. But her mother, Elizabeth Smith, wouldn't let her or her ladylike sister Mary, age twelve, go. (Abigail's little sister, Betsy, age three, was too young to think about school.) Mrs. Smith feared the girls might get sick, and anyway, girls could learn everything they needed to know right at home.

Abby, who knew girls were every bit as smart as boys, watched sadly as William strutted off to school by himself.

By the time Abigail was ten, she knew how to make soap, candles, bread, pudding, and pumpkin pies. She knew how to milk cows and churn butter, how to spin wool, weave cloth, knit mittens and stockings, and do plain and fancy sewing. She even knew how to cook snails, worms, and salt to make medicine. She watched her mother care for the sick, poor, and old people in their town, and she expected to follow this same "path of duty."

Abigail's father was a graduate of Harvard College. He told Abby her fine mind was a gift from God, to be filled with book learning (at home). So when she was not helping her mother or acting wild, she was in her father's large library, running her fingers over the books, pulling them off the shelves, reading and learning.

And often, to her mother's relief, she was at her grandparents' house. Abigail's grandparents, John and Elizabeth Quincy, lived four miles from the Smith farm. Abby loved to visit them, and she often stayed there for weeks at a time, reading and learning even more.

Grandfather's library was even larger than her father's. Abigail's dark eyes sparkled as she chose books from his tall shelves and carefully turned the thin pages. In the evenings, she sat with Grandmother by the flickering fire and tried to make the tiny stitches in her needlework come out just right, while Grandfather read the latest newspapers from England to them.

Grandfather had many important visitors, and Abby always wanted to hear what they were saying. Usually, if she sat quietly on her stool in the corner, they forgot a little girl was there at all. So Abby was as silent as the moonlight slanting across the floor.

In 1755, when Abby was eleven, Grandfather's visitors were talking about the war between France and England over which one of the countries would own North America. What if France won and took over the English colonies, Abby wondered. Then what? What was King George II doing about this back in England? Would England win? (England won.)

Abby read more about these problems in her father's newspapers at home, and listened to his visitors, too. She began thinking unladylike thoughts about how best to run a country. And sometimes she said what she thought—right in front of Parson Smith's visitors.

Her mother despaired. Women were not supposed to have opinions about things outside the home, or if they had them, they certainly shouldn't *say* them. Mary and Betsy were sweet and quiet daughters who could be guided by a thread, Mrs. Smith said, but Abigail required a heavy rope.

Abby really wanted to be a good girl like her sisters. But she kept on reading, thinking, and saying exactly what she thought.

As she grew older, Abigail was allowed to visit her aunt and uncle in Boston. Uncle Isaac Smith, her father's brother, was a rich ship owner. His big house was so close to Boston Harbor that Abigail could see tall-masted sailing ships from the window and smell the whale oil and ropes and tar on the long wharf that stuck out into the harbor. Buggy wheels and iron horseshoes clanged on Boston's crooked cobblestone streets. Shopkeepers shouted. Church bells rang from tall steeples. The whole town was exciting, Abby thought.

In Boston and at home in Weymouth, Abby had lots of friends—but no young men courted her. They thought she knew too much and had too many opinions. Abby didn't care. Don't wait for me to have a sweetheart, she told her cousin, because you'll be old and blind before I do.

Then, when she was sixteen, Abby met John Adams, age twenty-five, a stuffy young lawyer who enjoyed a good argument. (John had come to Parson Smith's farm with his friend Richard Cranch, who was engaged to Abigail's sister Mary.) Abigail was short and slender, with flashing black eyes, a strong chin, and a quick wit. John was short and chubby, and he wasn't afraid of a young lady who was as smart as he was.

John *liked* arguing with Abigail. He began stopping at the Smith farm as often as he could.

Abigail's mother was most unhappy about these visits. She thought John was too short, too plump, too rude, and too poor for her daughter. But Abigail and John were a good match, and they liked each other more and more. They began to talk about a life together.

Abigail thought long and hard about marrying John. She loved him, and she knew he loved her. The problem was the law of marriage.

Marriage made one person out of two, and by law that person was the husband. A wife could not own anything, not even her clothes. Women were told, from "the day you marry you must have no will of your own." And who made this ridiculous law? Men, of course.

But in the fall of 1763, Abigail's worries about marriage were set aside by a deadly smallpox epidemic in Boston. John was in danger because he rode to Boston often to work on his law cases.

The only answer was inoculation, a new treatment that infected a person with enough of the smallpox to make him sick, but not enough to kill him. (That was the idea, anyway.) John decided to go to Boston for the five-week treatment.

Abigail wrote to him every day. "Be careful," she wrote, "good folks are scarce." She knew now that honest, upright John Adams was the life partner for her, worth the risk of marriage, and she counted the days until he could return. "To morrow makes the 14th Day," she wrote. "How many more are to come? I dare not trust my self with the thought."

John wrote, too, and called her "Miss Adorable." One day he sent Miss Adorable a list of her faults— she hadn't learned to sing or play cards, she didn't sit up straight, and she sat with her legs crossed.

Lady.

John's inoculation was successful. (He was a little sick, but not too sick.) He hurried back to Abigail, and they eagerly set the date for their wedding.

Abigail began sewing new clothes, sheets, and tablecloths. John began fixing up his house. Finally everything was ready.

They were married on October 25, 1764. John was twenty-nine. Abigail was nineteen.

2

King George's New Rules

Abigail moved into John's plain wooden house in Braintree, right across the road from John's mother, Susanna, and only five miles from Weymouth.

Abigail loved her new home. There was just enough room for John's study and a sitting room on the first floor, with a kitchen and a huge brick fireplace for cooking in back of the house. Narrow stairs went up to two bedrooms and the attic.

She hung her yellow straw bonnet on a hook and got right to work. She put their new bed warmer (a wedding gift) by the fireplace in the bedroom, so she could fill it with hot coals and warm the sheets on icy nights. She had the furniture put just where she wanted it. She chose the spot for her garden, and crunched through reddish-gold autumn leaves on her way back and forth to the barn and chicken coop.

She had one servant, on loan from John's mother, to help with the cleaning and washing, the chickens, cows, and garden. Abigail did the cooking and sewing, because she thought she did it better than anyone else. Often, as she shelled peas for dinner, she talked with John and his friends.

That winter John had to ride through the snow to other towns to practice law (called "riding circuit"), but every evening when he was home they sat together beside the fire to drink their tea. They read the *Boston Gazette* and books from John's library. Abi-

Abigail's first baby was born on a hot Sunday morning in July 1765. They named their little girl Abigail, but called her Nabby to prevent mix-ups.

Meanwhile, back in England, King George thought of another new rule. His American colonists would have to pay for specially stamped paper from England, and they had to use this stamped paper for any business.

But the colonists had no vote in England on how their Stamp Tax money was spent. So John and other colonists wrote articles saying this rule was wrong.

We are *English*men, they said, not slaves without any rights.

Abigail and John talked about what they should do. It was their duty, they agreed, to *not* buy this stamped paper, even if business stopped. Other colonists did the same. Business stopped. No ships sailed from the colonies to England.

In the spring of 1766, King George gave up. The Stamp Tax was canceled. Business resumed, ships sailed, law courts reopened, and John went back to work. The thirteen colonies were peaceful once again. Abigail was happy and content, especially when her second baby, John Quincy, was born in 1767.

But in England, King George was being scolded by his mother. Be a *king,* George, she said. George decided he'd try again to show the colonists who was in charge. He put taxes on tea, glass, paint, and paper.

So Abigail served coffee, not tea. She did without glass and paint. She couldn't do without paper, though. John was often away, riding circuit, and Abigail needed lots of paper to write all her thoughts to him. "Dearest of Friends," her letters to John began.

John was so busy with work in Boston that they decided to move there in the spring of 1768. Abigail knew that John also wanted to help solve the colonists' problems with King George, and he could do this best from Boston.

Abigail packed books and clothes, furniture and bedding, food and firewood, and John found a man to watch the farm. They rented a pleasant white house on Brattle Square, a quiet green park that was not quiet for long.

King George was unhappy that the colonists had stopped buying glass and paint and tea, so he sent British troops to Boston to make them obey his rules. The troops practiced their marching on Brattle Square every morning, with thundering drums, screeching whistles, and tramping feet—right under Abigail and John's windows.

Every day Abigail bundled up Nabby, age three, and Johnny, age one, and took them for a walk. Every day they saw more and more British soldiers in their bright red coats.

How sad, she thought. We only want to live as peaceful citizens of England, as we always have. Trouble was coming. She just didn't know when.

In December 1768, Abigail's third baby was born —a girl, named Susanna for John's mother. But Susanna was not as healthy as Nabby and Johnny. She died when she was one year old, and Abigail's heart ran over with grief.

By 1770, after two years of marching and drumming, the soldiers and the colonists were tired of each other. England, Abigail said sadly, is a cruel mother country.

On the moonlit night of March 5, 1770, while John was at a meeting, Abigail heard gunfire and shouting in the streets. Church bells clanged loudly. She told Nabby and Johnny to stay in bed while she watched at the window for John, who soon burst into the house with the news. Some men and boys had thrown snowballs at the soldiers, he said, and the soldiers fired back. Five colonists were killed.

She shuddered at John's words. Trouble was here.

In June, John was chosen as a delegate to the Massachusetts Assembly. He was proud of this honor and of the chance to work even harder on the colonists' problems with King George—but Abigail cried while they talked it over.

Their fourth baby, a boy they named Charles, was only one week old, and Abigail was afraid. If John took this position, he would have less time for his own work. They might run out of money. Worse, John might be in trouble with the king, who was already angry with the colonists. Worst of all, the king might say John (and the other patriots, too) was a traitor to England—and *hang* him.

But John thought he should do his duty as an American and be a delegate. Abigail knew about duty. She dried her tears and told John she would stand with him in whatever was to come, and trust in God.

They stayed in Boston for one more year. Then they decided they'd had enough of city life and soldiers and drums. What they really needed was country air, so in April 1771 they moved back to their peaceful farm.

When Abigail saw their rocky tree-covered hills again, she sighed with happiness. She milked her cows and patted them tenderly. She made butter, planted vegetables, and baked bread and spicy puddings in her big brick fireplace. But John had to ride to Boston and back every day, and even though he had a fast horse, he wasn't getting his work done. So after a year, he bought a house in Boston just opposite the Court House, and Abigail packed again.

Her fifth baby, Thomas, was born in September 1772. In November she returned to Boston with Nabby, age seven; Johnny, age five; Charles, age two; baby Tommy; and her farm carts piled high with pumpkins, onions, turnips, and firewood.

That winter and all the next summer, Boston was peaceful. But back in England, George's mother was still scolding. Be a *king,* George! she said again.

In the autumn of 1773, King George decided to act kinglike by telling the colonists, who had stopped buying tea, that he was sending tea anyway. The colonists *must* buy it and pay tax on it, too, he said.

We won't, the colonists said.

On December 5, 1773, Abigail wrote to a friend that the tea, and trouble, had arrived. "What a pitty it is," she wrote, "that we can die but once to save our Country."

Eleven days later a group of colonists disguised as Mohawk Indians climbed onto the tea ships. They chopped open 342 boxes of tea and threw every tea leaf into Boston Harbor. Then they disappeared into the cold, rainy night.

King George heard about the Boston Tea Party. He was not pleased. To punish the colonists, he sent more troops to control them and closed Boston Harbor.

Abigail thought her family would be safer back on the farm, close to John's mother and to her sister Mary Cranch. She hurriedly packed again.

Riders galloped from colony to colony, carrying news from Boston. Men from all thirteen colonies were chosen to meet in Philadelphia, to solve the colonies' problems with King George. John was one of those chosen men, and Abigail's life changed forever.

3

John's Duty

In August 1774, Abigail waved good-bye to John as he and four other delegates to the First Continental Congress set off on the hot and dusty ride to Philadelphia. Her heart overflowed with pride in John *and* worry about the future. There will be war, she thought, if we want to be free from England.

She had always been in charge of the house, the children, the garden, and the dairy. Now, with John away, she would take his side of the partnership, too. She would be in charge of the whole farm, all the animals, the tenants who rented farmland from John, John's law clerks, and the family's income until John returned.

While she worked, Abigail had seven-year-old Johnny read aloud to her and Nabby from thick books on Greek and Roman history. Johnny learned to read, and they all learned how other countries made laws.

And if she wasn't busy enough already, John sent her a long letter that ended, "It is time, my Dear, for you to begin to teach them French."

Abigail had not received that letter when she wrote to John in September. "Dearest Friend," she said, "Five Weeks have past and not one line have I received." She told him that people were worried about war. She also described a problem she kept thinking about—slavery in America—a problem that few other people, except for the slaves themselves, thought about. The colonies might soon be fighting for freedom from England, she said, but in the southern colonies the slaves were not free. How can we fight, she wrote John, "for what we are daily robbing . . . from those who have as good a right to freedom as we have"?

"My Much Loved Friend," she wrote in October, "I long for your return." And, she wrote, people at home have no idea what you and the other men in the First Continental Congress are doing.

So Abigail told them herself. She told her family, friends at dinner parties, people in town, and visitors at her door that the men in Philadelphia were trying to save the rights American colonists had always had as Englishmen. The men were trying, Abigail said, to convince King George not to send more soldiers, more tea, or more rules.

John, meanwhile, wrote that he was having a hard time getting anything done. If I said to Congress, he wrote, "that Three and two make five," it would take two days of talking before the men would agree on it.

John finally came home in November 1774, to a farm that was as neat as a newly made bed, to the children jumping around him like puppies, and to Abigail, pleased and proud. Her family was together again and the farm was safe, she thought, from the thousands of British soldiers only ten miles away in Boston.

In the spring, as the snow on Abigail and John's farm melted and the pastures turned green, seven hundred red-coated British soldiers marched north out of Boston toward Concord, thirty miles from Braintree. The rising sun sparkled on their guns. They marched in orderly lines, straight for the guns that the colonists had been hiding in Concord.

But the minutemen (colonists who could be ready to fight in a minute) had been warned. They rushed from their farms. Some minutemen were shot and killed. Others fired back and killed some of the soldiers. The surprised redcoats hurried back to Boston. The colonists were going to fight!

When Abigail heard that fighting with England had begun, she shivered with a little fear, and a lot of excitement. She was now, she said, "a daughter of America."

In May 1775, John left again for Philadelphia. Abigail and the children stayed on the farm, but it was no longer quiet. Families fleeing from the British in Boston passed by Abigail's farmhouse, and they brought bad news. Houses in Boston, including Abigail and John's house, had been taken over by British soldiers.

The refugees from Boston stayed with Abigail, some for a day or a night, some for a week. Minutemen stopped for food and rest. Abigail sighed, thinking of the places she had put people—the barn, the attic, the parlor floor.

Saturday morning, June 17, Abigail sewed and listened to Nabby and Johnny read their French lessons. Suddenly the house shook, and they heard a tremendous boom. Pictures swung crazily on the whitewashed walls.

All day the house rattled and shivered with the thunder of guns and heavy cannons. Late in the afternoon, Abigail took Johnny by the hand. They walked quickly to the top of Penn's Hill, where they could see all the way to Boston.

They saw American cannons on a hill just across the river from Boston, firing into Boston, and British cannons firing back. Abigail didn't even try to wipe away the tears running down her cheeks as they watched Boston's church steeples turn into great towers of flame.

The next afternoon, the cannons still boomed. Abigail collected all her pewter spoons and took them to the kitchen. John's brother Elihu, a minuteman, was there, his musket across his back. They put the spoons into a large kettle over the fire. As Abigail's precious spoons melted, Elihu molded the pewter into bullets—fifteen bullets from each pound of pewter. Abigail saw Johnny standing silently in the doorway, watching. She smiled, so he'd know she was proud to be doing this, but she couldn't speak.

She wrote to John every day and told him what was happening at home. She told him people were impatient for Congress to *do* something. She asked John if the men of Congress had any idea how the people were suffering.

"No," John wrote back. "They cant, they dont."

Abigail filled her letters with so much news that John called her his "home-front reporter." Because of her letters, John, more than any other man in Congress, knew what ordinary Americans were thinking.

Then, Congress finally did something. When John suggested that George Washington, a Virginian who had led troops in the French and Indian War, would be the best man to lead a new American army, Congress agreed. George Washington, John wrote to Abigail, is "one of the most important Characters in the World."

In the middle of July, General Washington himself stopped at Abigail's farmhouse. He invited her to visit the army camp and stay for dinner. After the dinner, Abigail wrote to John that Washington was indeed a Godlike figure, "built by hands divine." She had dinner with the famous Benjamin Franklin, too, and talked with men traveling to Philadelphia.

This was not turning out to be the life she had expected. But she believed that John was doing what only he, and a very few other men, could do. John Adams was helping to create a new nation. This was more important than her own or the children's happiness. However long John was away, Abigail would do both the woman's and the man's work in their partnership. This would be, she decided, her sacrifice to her country. (It would also show that a woman was the equal of a man.)

4

A New Nation

In the fall of 1775, Abigail, three-year-old Tommy, and many others came down with an awful disease called dysentery. "I set down with a heavy Heart to write to you," a weak and tearful Abigail wrote on September 25. John's brother Elihu and Elihu's little son were dead, and she herself was so sick that her mother, Elizabeth, came every day to care for her and for Tommy. Then her mother fell ill.

Abigail and Tommy recovered. But in October, her mother died. "How can I tell you," she wrote John through her tears, "that my Dear Mother has left me." Abigail had often told her sisters that a cheerful heart was the best medicine. Now Abigail needed a large dose of that medicine.

In November, rain and snow ruined hundreds of apples Abigail had planned to use for her favorite cider. There would be no cider, but there were still lessons to teach and clothes to make for Nabby, age ten; Johnny, age eight; Charles, age five; and Tommy, age three. There were crops to sell, cows to milk—and Abigail was getting annoyed.

What is Congress *doing?* she wrote John impatiently. It's time to *separate* from England. "I wish I knew what mighty things" are going on, she wrote. What kind of laws would they make? Would they have a monarchy or a democracy?

The ground was still covered with snow in March 1776 when the Americans moved their cannons to a hill south of Boston, near Abigail's farmhouse. The cannons fired all night from the American lines into Boston, as steady as a heartbeat. "No sleep for me tonight," Abigail wrote to John as her desk shook.

The cannons kept firing, and lines of American soldiers marched past the farmhouse on their way to Boston. When the firing stopped a week later, those American soldiers stood on the hills overlooking Boston. The British soldiers, taken by surprise, left Boston in defeat. General Washington had his first victory. Now, Abigail wrote happily, the sun shone brighter and the birds sang more sweetly.

The men in Philadelphia were talking about a new government for America. It was the right time to make new laws for women, too, Abigail thought. Under the old English law, a woman had no property or rights of her own, but now new laws could be made

34

that would treat American women the same as American men. She immediately wrote to John.

"I long to hear that you have declared an independancy," she wrote, "and by the way in the new Code of Laws...I desire you would Remember the Ladies." Women should not be ruled by laws they did not make, she said, most firmly.

"As to your extraordinary Code of Laws," John answered, "I cannot but laugh.... We [men] know better," he wrote, than to give up our power.

"I can not say that I think you very generous to the Ladies," Abigail wrote back stubbornly, "for whilst you are proclaiming peace and good will to Men," you keep "absolute power over Wives."

She was cross with John and impatient with Congress. It's as if, she said, the building is on fire and Congress argues about the cost of the water to put the fire out. The king is no longer our king, she said. Why not tell the world?

Abigail hardly knew whether to laugh or cry each time John sent another list of instructions (train the children to be decent and honest, "fire them with Ambition to be usefull," make the boys "great and manly"). What did he *think* she was doing?

She also sold milk, butter, and grain to pay John's taxes and for John's house in Boston. When everything was paid, she wrote, "it gives me great pleasure to say they are done."

John wrote back that he feared the neighbors would think she took better care of things than he did. (She did.)

In July 1776, Abigail, her two sisters, and all the children went to Uncle Isaac's house in Boston for smallpox inoculations, because the deadly disease was spreading all over New England.

At the very same time, thanks to John Adams's arguments (with the information from Abigail's letters), the men in Philadelphia finally made up their minds to tell the world the king was no longer their king. Thomas Jefferson told the world why, in the Declaration of Independence.

On July 13, 1776, in Boston, Abigail received John's joyful letter telling her that the most memorable day in the history of America had occurred. It was the Fourth of July, a day to be celebrated with parades, bells, and fireworks "from this Time forward."

At the end of July, after a church service, Abigail stood in an excited crowd and heard the Declaration read from the balcony of the State House in Boston. And *you,* she wrote John proudly, "had the Honour of being a principal actor in laying a foundation" for America.

Now there was a new reason to let American girls go to school. "If we mean to have Heroes, Statesmen, and Philosophers," she wrote to John, "we should have learned women." Women must be educated so they can best teach their children, she said, and she planned to keep on saying it.

Early in September 1776, she and the children, all healthy, returned to the farm. John came home, too, for a short visit.

When spring came, nine-year-old Johnny rode to Boston on his little brown mare, taking his mother's letters to the post rider there and bringing his father's letters back to Braintree. Abigail laughed when he slowly pulled letters out of his pockets, one by one, to tease her. She missed John more than ever, because she was expecting their sixth baby. John wrote that he was lonely, too. Future Americans had better appreciate their sacrifices, he wrote, "and make a good Use of it." They "will never know, how much it cost" us.

But Abigail wanted John, not his letters. She wrote him that even *animals* had a mate to "sit by them."

"Oh that I could be near," John wrote. But he was three hundred miles away.

Her baby, a girl, was born dead. Eleven-year-old Nabby wept for her dead sister, and Abigail cried with her. Then she wrote John the sad, sad news.

Two weeks later, 260 British ships and 15,000 British soldiers were seen near Boston. Again, Americans fled from Boston. Again, John was not home.

He wasn't in Philadelphia either. British troops captured Philadelphia, and John and all the men of Congress had to pack their papers and run for their lives.

Abigail kept writing. She told John that her farmworker had left in the middle of haying to join the army. She told him American money wasn't good anymore, so she traded her farm goods for wool, salt, and sugar. She said she heard that American soldiers were retreating because they had no gunpowder. How can this be? she asked John.

She wrote to John on their thirteenth wedding anniversary in October and reminded him that he had been away for three years (except for a month or two here and there). She had been patient, she said, because he was serving their country, but her patience was running out. She had sacrificed enough.

In November, John resigned from Congress and hurried home. Abigail was rosy with contentment again. She did her work, John did his work, and the children tagged after them. All was well—for one month.

5

Europe

On December 15, 1777, John was in New Hampshire working on a law case when a letter from Congress arrived. Abigail opened it, thinking it might be urgent news for John, and sank into her chair in horror. A Mr. Lovell asked John to go three thousand miles across the Atlantic Ocean to France, to help Benjamin Franklin get French guns and men for America's army. Abigail couldn't believe it.

She didn't wait for John's return. She wrote to Mr. Lovell at once. How could you "rob me of all my happiness?" she cried angrily. But she knew the American army was shivering in snow-covered tents at Valley Forge, Pennsylvania. She knew the men needed guns, food, clothes, and shoes. And she knew what John would say.

John said he would go. It was his duty.

Ten-year-old Johnny wanted to go, too. Abigail was terrified that he might die at sea, or forget his duty to do right, but she agreed. It was her duty.

She began to get them ready. She packed pipes and pens, ink, paper, and books; food and clothes; and she sent a cow, sheep, chickens, and corn. In February, 1778, Abigail said good-bye to her husband again and to her oldest son for the very first time. She kissed them and watched through her tears until they were out of sight. "I asked not my Heart what it could [do]," she wrote to a friend, "but what it ought to do."

Now Abigail became a businesswoman. American money was just "blank paper," and she needed objects to trade, to pay the bills. She sent John lists of things (calico with pretty flowers, ribbons, fancy lace, colorful handkerchiefs, fans, coffeepots, pudding dishes) he could buy in Paris and send to her. She traded French dishes for flour or sugar or whatever she needed. She sold French lace and ribbons in a friend's store to people with good money (British sterling) and paid John's taxes with sterling.

She rented out John's farmland (without asking John). And she sent Nabby, now thirteen, to school (without asking John). "I concluded to put out the Farm," she wrote after she'd done it, adding, "Our daughter is at School in Boston."

The next winter's snowdrifts melted. Spring came and went.

One morning in August 1779, Abigail looked up from her work and saw a man and a boy walking up the road. She dropped her sewing to the floor and with a cry of joy flew out the door, into John's arms.

The small farmhouse was crowded with John's boxes of books, but the six Adamses were small, too. They all fit nicely together—for a few weeks.

In October, Congress asked John to go back to Paris to work on the peace treaty between America and England. It was an honor he wanted very much. It was his duty to go, he said.

In November, John and twelve-year-old Johnny sailed back to Europe. Charles, age nine, went with them. Johnny hadn't wanted to cross the ocean again, and Charles didn't want to go at all, but Abigail said it would be good for them. It was her duty to send them, she said.

When she was alone, Abigail read the note John had given her before he sailed. "We shall yet be happy," he had written. She wanted to believe it, but she wasn't sure anymore.

She wrote to Johnny, reminding him to watch his temper. Your duty, she told him, is to God, society, country, parents, and yourself—and in that order.

"These are times," she said, "in which a Genious would wish to live." She told lovable, blond, curly-haired Charles to be useful and happy. She wrote John how to instruct the boys. Don't teach them what to think, but *how* to think, she said. Then she went back to work.

Eight months later, she heard that Benjamin Franklin had written to Congress, saying John was a bad diplomat. (True, John Adams was stubborn, prickly, and tactless.) Then she heard that because of Franklin's letter Congress was sending three more men to Paris, including Thomas Jefferson, to work with John on a peace treaty.

Abigail was furious for John's sake. She knew how much this would hurt him, because he wanted the honor of making the treaty alone. She wrote angrily to Lovell. She had given her best years so John could serve his country, she said, and "when he is wounded I blead."

She wrote to John. Don't resign because of what Franklin said, she said. Be firm, and don't be hurt. Also, she added, send "some small present from your own Hand" to your mother.

John was still gone when the British surrendered to General Washington at Yorktown, Virginia. It was October 1781. The Revolutionary War was over.

Abigail was so excited she could hardly sit still, and her pen flew exuberantly across the page. America has done, she said, "what no power before her ever did"—defeated the British Empire in battle.

Six months later John still was not home. "Let me beg of you to resign," Abigail wrote to him in March 1782. (Homesick Charles, age eleven, had returned by himself in January. It took him five months and several ships.)

In September 1783, the peace treaty with England was signed. John still was not home. He was working on business deals for the new United States and knew he wouldn't be home soon. He wrote to Abigail, "Will you come to me this Fall? . . . I am so unhappy without you."

As Abigail read John's letter over and over, her throat tightened with fear. She had never been more than forty miles from home. What would Europeans think of her? What if the ship sank? What about her family?

She decided to go. John could use her help, and she could learn how women were educated in Europe. Besides, she wanted to see John again.

She found people to help with the farm. Her sister Mary would care for John's aged mother, and her sister Betsy took Charles and Tommy into her home. Nabby, eighteen, agreed to go with her mother.

In July 1784, Abigail and Nabby arrived in England. When their carriage stopped in front of Lows Hotel in London, Abigail looked eagerly for John.

He wasn't there. She sighed, rented rooms, and took out her pen and paper.

Three days later, in Holland, John received her letter. "Your Letter of the 23d has made me the happiest Man upon Earth," he wrote back.

John Quincy got to London before his father did. Abigail threw her arms around him, kissed him, and wept for joy. She had not seen her son since he was twelve years old. Now he was a grown-up young man of seventeen.

John arrived one week later, and he and Abigail flew to each other like magnets. She wrote to her sister Mary, "we were indeed a very very happy family once more."

They moved to Paris for John's work, where Abigail became good friends with Thomas Jefferson. Abigail loved a good discussion, and she spoke freely with Jefferson. They talked about everything from books to politics.

Then Congress appointed John as the first American ambassador to England, and the Adams family moved back to London. Abigail was thrilled at this new honor for John, although, she wrote to Mary,

"I shall really regret to leave Mr. Jefferson."

John couldn't wait to show his former king and enemy, George III, that the rebellious American colonies had become an important country. He enjoyed being at the king's royal court.

Abigail didn't.

When she was presented to the king and queen, Abigail wore a white dress covered with ribbons and ruffles, with more ruffles and feathers on her cap. She thought she looked like a ship in full sail, and she felt ridiculous. She had wanted a simple dress, and she thought it was silly to stand in a crowded room for hours just to curtsy to someone.

She preferred to have people come for fine dinners at her home. To save money, she did the shopping and cooking herself. This was common sense to Abigail, but the London papers made fun of it. When she read the papers she thought longingly of her farm back home.

In London, though, she finally got to go to school, to hear some lectures on science. "It was like going into a beautifull Country which I never saw before," she wrote Mary excitedly, and she said (again) that America *must* have educated women.

John Quincy needed to finish his education, so he returned to America to go to Harvard University.

Nabby stayed in London and married Colonel William Smith, John's secretary.

Abigail and John decided they would need a larger home when they returned to America. By mail, they bought a house in Braintree, close to Mary and Richard's house, and Abigail sent directions for fixing it up.

When John's work in London came to an end, Abigail wrote to Jefferson in Paris to tell him good-bye. She'd rather be home with her chickens, she said, than with the queen of England.

(Nabby was returning to America, too, but on a different ship. She and Colonel Smith and their new baby would live in New York, far from Abigail and John.)

In June 1788, Abigail and John's ship sailed into Boston Harbor. Abigail gasped when she saw thousands of people lining the docks to greet them. Cannons roared in welcome, church bells rang, and best of all, John Quincy, Charles, Tommy, and Mary Cranch and her family were there.

After the welcoming speeches, the Adamses set out for their new home.

It wasn't as big as Abigail had expected. In fact, it seemed as small as "a wren's nest," and it was filled with noise and dust. Their furniture arrived, wet and broken. There were piles of books, but no book-shelves. John bought six cows for Abigail's dairy, but there was no barn. And the kitchen was too small.

All summer they worked. By the end of 1788, they were ready to enjoy their house and farm. Abigail thought they would never move again.

6

A New Government

Early in 1789, the first leaders of the United States were chosen by Congress. George Washington was elected president, and Abigail's dear John was elected vice president.

She felt warm with happiness at this great honor for John. True, they would have to move to New York City, the capital, but duty came first.

She worried that she might act differently now that she was the wife of the vice president, so she asked her sisters to warn her if she did. It's easy, she said, to think we're better than we really are.

The new leaders didn't know how to act, either. Vice President Adams wondered if he should sit or stand when he presided over the Senate. The senators wondered if they should sit or stand when the president arrived. They soon solved the problem. When President Washington stood, they all stood. When President Washington sat, they all sat.

The Adamses went to the first dinner given by Martha Washington. The dining room was hot with candles, fourteen guests, nervous waiters, and footmen standing stiffly behind each chair. But the meal was eaten in total silence, for no one, not even Abigail, dared to speak before President Washington spoke. And he never spoke.

Abigail and Martha were anxious to set just the right tone for the new government (that first dinner wasn't quite right). They carefully planned proper social evenings, one for each night of the week.

For her evenings, Abigail fixed little cakes, dressed confidently in a richly colored dress trimmed with heavy lace and her best fancy slippers with low heels, and covered her hair with a fashionable cap. Ladies and gentlemen came, bowed politely, talked solemnly, ate the little cakes, drank tea, bowed again, and left. Abigail loved good, sensible talk and an argument or two. She found these proper social evenings as dull as cabbage.

But she was excited about John's work as vice president and her duties as his wife. When newspapers began to print articles by men who disagreed with John and who made fun of the way he dressed, talked, and acted, she was shocked. She couldn't understand why Americans, the people John had worked so hard for, would write unkind things about him. She wrote to friends, told them what John was doing, and asked them to write kind articles for the papers.

Abigail worried that she couldn't pay their bills. "I fear we shall not make both ends meet," she wrote Mary (but she always sent money to the poor in Braintree). She worried about Nabby, Nabby's children, Charles, Tommy, and her niece Louisa. (They all lived with Abigail, and someone was always sick.) She worried about their differences with Thomas Jefferson, who was secretary of state. When she saw a newspaper article in 1791 in which Jefferson said John's ideas for the country were wrong, she was outraged. She decided he was no longer a friend.

By 1796, after eight years as president, George Washington wanted to retire.

John wanted to be the next president. He considered being vice president again, perhaps under Thomas Jefferson, who also wanted to be president. But Abigail thought John should not be second to any man except Washington. President or nothing, she advised. She worried, though, that the next president would be on a slippery slope surrounded by a quicksand of problems. She was right.

She worried that she wouldn't be a proper First Lady because she wasn't as quiet and gentle as

Martha Washington was. She wrote John that she knew she talked too much. John wrote back, "A Woman *can* be silent, when she will." The problem was, Abigail didn't will it. She had too much to say.

It was a bitter election. The brand-new country was already divided. Some, like Adams, thought the country should be run by educated upper-class men who knew what was best for ordinary people. Others, like Jefferson, thought educated ordinary people (farmers would be best) could run their own country.

On February 8, 1797, John Adams was elected president. Thomas Jefferson came in second and was the vice president.

In March 1797, in the new capital city of Philadelphia, John was sworn in as president of the United States. Abigail was sick at home in Quincy (the new name for Braintree) on the biggest day of their life, and not one of their children attended. That night John wrote sadly in his diary, "It would have given me great pleasure to have some of my family present." Then he immediately wrote Abigail, "I must have you here to assist me. I can do nothing without you."

But she couldn't leave Quincy until she found money for their taxes. (When the tax collector heard that, he said if the *president* couldn't pay, "who could?")

She paid the taxes, squeezed family and servants

into two carriages, and splashed through rain and mud for one week. On the way to Philadelphia, she wrote her prayer as First Lady. "May I do my part with honor," she began.

She got right to work on her part. She helped John with his speeches and papers. She had dinners for thirty to forty people every week. But some newspapers said she wasted money on parties. Other newspapers sneered that she didn't give *enough* parties. Abigail was surprised and hurt at the papers' "lies [and] falsehoods" about her and about John.

President Adams was soon sinking in a quicksand of problems. There was trouble with France, trouble with England, and trouble at home.

Some newspapers made fun of the short, chubby president by calling him "His Rotundity." Other papers printed cruel jokes about John's work. When Abigail read that Benjamin Franklin's grandson called her John "old, bald, blind, crippled, toothless Adams," her spirits sank with bitterness. Was this the thanks they got, after giving up their happiness for their country?

Things were worse in 1799. Many Americans wanted the president to declare war on France, but John wanted to settle the differences peacefully. Nabby's husband suddenly left for England without her, leaving her in a lonely log cabin thirty miles outside New York. Nabby felt too discouraged to care for her two sons, so Abigail's sister Betsy took them in. And Abigail's lovable Charles was sinking into drink and depression in New York.

Abigail was sick in Quincy and felt depressed herself. But when she read a book that said women were less important than men, she snatched up her pen and wrote a fiery letter to Betsy. I will *never* allow women to be considered as less than men, she said, again.

At the beginning of December 1799, she was back in Philadelphia. President Adams was still trying to avoid war with France, and to Abigail and John's surprise, people cheered him! He made a speech that received "more applause . . . than any speech which the President has ever before delivered," Abigail wrote happily to Mary.

But at the end of December, George Washington died, and John's work for peace was forgotten. People talked about what a great man Washington had been. President Adams was not as great, they said. Abigail tried to ignore this talk. "Gloom is no part of my Religion," she said.

She did feel gloomy, though, and not only about politics. Charles was drinking himself to death. In

November 1800, she went to New York to see Charles again. He was terribly sick. Abigail hurt with sadness for her son, and she bought his daughters into her household.

She went on to meet John in Washington, the brand-new capital city. Abigail was miserable, and so was her trip to Washington. The coachman got lost in the woods. The horses trotted on, with the carriage breaking tree branches right and left. When the carriage finally slid to a stop in the mud in front of the President's House, Abigail was astonished. It was a castle in a muddy swamp, surrounded by shacks, bricks, and trash.

Not one room of the President's House was finished. Abigail had thirteen fireplaces going every day to dry the damp plaster, fresh paint, and wet laundry, and to keep her family and visitors somewhat warm and comfortable. She bought dozens of candles, some elegant furniture, and tried to make the house suitable for a president.

John Adams and Thomas Jefferson both ran for president in the 1800 election. This time, Jefferson won. Abigail was sad for John, who had been an honest, upright—and stubborn and unpopular—president.

Charles died. Christmas came and went, while Abigail grieved for her sweet son.

One week later, she gave her last party in the President's House. She had the fireplaces blazing and the tables ready, and she greeted her guests with a smile. (I dislike a groaning, whining, complaining person, she said.)

After the party, Abigail packed for the very last time, gathered her large family of children and grandchildren, and set off for home. The carriages slid over frozen rivers and snowy roads as the horses trotted along, blowing clouds of steamy breath. She laughed, thinking of her niece Louisa, who said Abigail should not travel in this weather (or ever) without a man to protect her. She had told Louisa kindly that she was used to getting through "many difficulties alone."

She had gotten through births, deaths, and the creation of a new country alone. She had done a man's work as well as a woman's. She believed in the right of women to be treated as equal to men, and she meant to keep saying what she thought. Abigail smiled as she thought of home, of all the reading and writing and ideas before her, of all the things she had yet to say, and of John, her Dearest Friend.

Afterword

Because Abigail had worked so hard and saved so carefully, she and John were able to live comfortably on their farm for the rest of their lives. Their children, grandchildren, nieces, nephews, and friends came often and stayed long. Abigail kept on taking care of her family, and she kept on writing letters. She kept on saying that women need education just as much as men do. She kept on arguing that women are the equal of men, each having different roles, and that women need equal protection under the law. Abigail's thoughts were ahead of her time—but her ideas and words helped shape a new nation in which women and men *do* have equal rights.

Abigail died at home in October 1818, with her Dearest Friend by her side.

Abigail Adams was not only the wife of one president. She was the mother of another. Her son, John Quincy Adams, was elected president of the United States in 1825.

Abigail's Dearest John died on July 4, 1826, the fiftieth anniversary of the Declaration of Independence. Thomas Jefferson, Abigail's old friend and foe, died on the very same day.

Selected Bibliography

Adams, Abigail. *The Book of Abigail and John: Selected Letters, 1762–1784.* Cambridge: Harvard Univ. Press, 1975.

——. *New Letters of Abigail Adams, 1788–1801.* Boston: Houghton Mifflin, 1947.

Adams, John. *Adams-Jefferson Letters.* 2 vols. New York: Simon & Schuster, 1971.

——. *The Adams Papers: Diary and Autobiography of John Adams.* Cambridge: Harvard Univ. Press, 1975.

Akers, Charles W. *Abigail Adams: An American Woman.* Boston: Little, Brown, 1980.

Bober, Natalie S. *Abigail Adams: Witness to a Revolution.* New York: Atheneum, 1995.

Boller, Paul F., Jr. *Presidential Wives.* New York: Oxford Univ. Press, 1988.

Gelles, Edith B. *Portia: The World of Abigail Adams.* Indianapolis: Indiana Univ. Press, 1992.

Levin, Phyllis Lee. *Abigail Adams: A Biography.* New York: Ballantine Books, 1987.

Shepherd, Jack. *The Adams Chronicles.* Boston: Little, Brown, 1975.

Websites

National First Ladies Library: Bibliography for Abigail Adams <www.firstladies.org/ABIGAIL_ADAMS/FL.html>

Birthplace of Abigail Adams <www.southshoreserver.com/abigailadams>

Index

George III (king of England), 18, 20, 21, 23, 24–25, 28, 48

Jefferson, Thomas, 36, 44, 47–48, 54, 55, 58, 61

London, England, 47, 48, 49

Minutemen. *See* American soldiers

New York City, 51

Paris, France, 47
Philadelphia, Pennsylvania, 55, 56, 57

Quincy, Elizabeth (grandmother), 9, 11
Quincy, John (grandfather), 11–12
Quincy, Massachusetts, 55, 57. *See also* Braintree

Revolutionary War, 28–32, 34–36, 39–40, 44–45

Smith, Abigail. *See* Adams, Abigail
Smith, Betsy (sister), 10, 12, 36, 45, 57

Smith, Elizabeth Quincy (mother), 10, 12, 15, 33
Smith, Mary (sister). *See* Cranch, Mary
Smith, William (brother), 10
Smith, William (father), 10, 12
Stamp Tax, 18, 20

Washington, D.C., 58
Washington, George, 32, 44, 51, 53, 54, 57
Washington, Martha, 53, 54–55
Weymouth, Massachusetts, 10, 13

JUV B ADA FERR   HO
Ferris, Jeri.
Remember the ladies

LAKE COUNTY PUBLIC LIBRARY
INDIANA

AD	FF	MU
AV	GR	NC
BO	HI	SJ
CL	HO AUG 21 '02	CNL
DS	LS	